CHECK /DEBIT CARD TRANSACTION REGISTER

NUMBERED FROM ____________ TO ____________

DATED FROM ________________ TO ____________

PROPERTY OF ________________________________

Date Range ______________________			Balance Brought Forward				$		
Debit/ Check Number	Date	Description of Transaction	√	Withdrawal Amount/ Debit		Deposit		Balance	

Date Range ______________________ Balance Brought Forward $

Debit/ Check Number	Date	Description of Transaction	√	Withdrawal Amount/ Debit		Deposit		Balance	

Date Range ______________________ | Balance Brought Forward | $

Debit/ Check Number	Date	Description of Transaction	√	Withdrawal Amount/ Debit		Deposit		Balance	

Date Range ____________________ Balance Brought Forward $

Debit/ Check Number	Date	Description of Transaction	√	Withdrawal Amount/ Debit		Deposit		Balance	

Date Range ____________________				Balance Brought Forward				$	
Debit/ Check Number	Date	Description of Transaction	√	Withdrawal Amount/ Debit		Deposit		Balance	

Date Range ____________			Balance Brought Forward					$	
Debit/ Check Number	Date	Description of Transaction	√	Withdrawal Amount/ Debit		Deposit		Balance	

Date Range ____________________				Balance Brought Forward				$	
Debit/ Check Number	Date	Description of Transaction	√	Withdrawal Amount/ Debit		Deposit		Balance	

Date Range ______________			Balance Brought Forward					$	
Debit/ Check Number	Date	Description of Transaction	√	Withdrawal Amount/ Debit		Deposit		Balance	

Date Range ______________________			Balance Brought Forward					$	
Debit/ Check Number	Date	Description of Transaction	√	Withdrawal Amount/ Debit		Deposit		Balance	

Date Range ______________________			Balance Brought Forward					$	
Debit/ Check Number	Date	Description of Transaction	√	Withdrawal Amount/ Debit		Deposit		Balance	

Date Range ________________ | Balance Brought Forward | $

Debit/ Check Number	Date	Description of Transaction	√	Withdrawal Amount/ Debit		Deposit		Balance	

Date Range ____________________				Balance Brought Forward				$	
Debit/ Check Number	Date	Description of Transaction	√	Withdrawal Amount/ Debit		Deposit		Balance	

Date Range ______________________ Balance Brought Forward $

Debit/ Check Number	Date	Description of Transaction	√	Withdrawal Amount/ Debit		Deposit		Balance	

Date Range ______________________				Balance Brought Forward				$	
Debit/ Check Number	Date	Description of Transaction	√	Withdrawal Amount/ Debit		Deposit		Balance	

Date Range ____________________ Balance Brought Forward $

Debit/ Check Number	Date	Description of Transaction	√	Withdrawal Amount/ Debit		Deposit		Balance	

Date Range ______________________			Balance Brought Forward					$	
Debit/ Check Number	Date	Description of Transaction	√	Withdrawal Amount/ Debit		Deposit		Balance	

Date Range ______________ Balance Brought Forward $

Debit/ Check Number	Date	Description of Transaction	√	Withdrawal Amount/ Debit		Deposit		Balance	

Date Range ______________________								Balance Brought Forward	$
Debit/ Check Number	Date	Description of Transaction	√	Withdrawal Amount/ Debit		Deposit		Balance	

Date Range ____________________				Balance Brought Forward				$	
Debit/ Check Number	Date	Description of Transaction	√	Withdrawal Amount/ Debit		Deposit		Balance	

Date Range ______________________				Balance Brought Forward			$		
Debit/ Check Number	Date	Description of Transaction	√	Withdrawal Amount/ Debit		Deposit		Balance	

Date Range ______________				Balance Brought Forward				$	
Debit/ Check Number	Date	Description of Transaction	√	Withdrawal Amount/ Debit		Deposit		Balance	

Date Range ____________				Balance Brought Forward				$	
Debit/ Check Number	Date	Description of Transaction	√	Withdrawal Amount/ Debit		Deposit		Balance	

Date Range ______________________				Balance Brought Forward				$	
Debit/ Check Number	Date	Description of Transaction	√	Withdrawal Amount/ Debit		Deposit		Balance	

Date Range ____________________	Balance Brought Forward	$

Debit/ Check Number	Date	Description of Transaction	√	Withdrawal Amount/ Debit		Deposit		Balance	

Date Range ________________			Balance Brought Forward					$	
Debit/ Check Number	Date	Description of Transaction	√	Withdrawal Amount/ Debit		Deposit		Balance	

Date Range ____________________ | Balance Brought Forward | $

Debit/ Check Number	Date	Description of Transaction	√	Withdrawal Amount/ Debit		Deposit		Balance	

Date Range ______________				Balance Brought Forward				$	
Debit/ Check Number	Date	Description of Transaction	√	Withdrawal Amount/ Debit		Deposit		Balance	

Date Range ______________________ Balance Brought Forward $

Debit/ Check Number	Date	Description of Transaction	√	Withdrawal Amount/ Debit		Deposit		Balance	

Date Range ______________________				Balance Brought Forward				$	
Debit/ Check Number	Date	Description of Transaction	√	Withdrawal Amount/ Debit		Deposit		Balance	

Date Range ____________________			Balance Brought Forward					$	
Debit/ Check Number	Date	Description of Transaction	√	Withdrawal Amount/ Debit		Deposit		Balance	

Date Range ______________			Balance Brought Forward					$	
Debit/ Check Number	Date	Description of Transaction	√	Withdrawal Amount/ Debit		Deposit		Balance	

Date Range ______________________	Balance Brought Forward	$

Debit/ Check Number	Date	Description of Transaction	√	Withdrawal Amount/ Debit		Deposit		Balance	

Date Range ________________				Balance Brought Forward				$	
Debit/ Check Number	Date	Description of Transaction	√	Withdrawal Amount/ Debit		Deposit		Balance	

Date Range ______________________			Balance Brought Forward					$	
Debit/ Check Number	Date	Description of Transaction	√	Withdrawal Amount/ Debit		Deposit		Balance	

Date Range ______________________ Balance Brought Forward $

Debit/ Check Number	Date	Description of Transaction	√	Withdrawal Amount/ Debit		Deposit		Balance	

Date Range ____________________				Balance Brought Forward				$	
Debit/ Check Number	Date	Description of Transaction	√	Withdrawal Amount/ Debit		Deposit		Balance	

Date Range ____________________				Balance Brought Forward				$	
Debit/ Check Number	Date	Description of Transaction	√	Withdrawal Amount/ Debit		Deposit		Balance	

Date Range ______________________	Balance Brought Forward	$

Debit/ Check Number	Date	Description of Transaction	√	Withdrawal Amount/ Debit		Deposit		Balance	

Date Range ______________			Balance Brought Forward					$	
Debit/ Check Number	Date	Description of Transaction	√	Withdrawal Amount/ Debit		Deposit		Balance	

Date Range ______________________ | Balance Brought Forward | $

Debit/ Check Number	Date	Description of Transaction	√	Withdrawal Amount/ Debit		Deposit		Balance	

Date Range ____________________ Balance Brought Forward $

Debit/ Check Number	Date	Description of Transaction	√	Withdrawal Amount/ Debit		Deposit		Balance	

Date Range ______________________ | Balance Brought Forward | $

Debit/ Check Number	Date	Description of Transaction	√	Withdrawal Amount/ Debit		Deposit		Balance	

Date Range ______________________ Balance Brought Forward $

Debit/ Check Number	Date	Description of Transaction	√	Withdrawal Amount/ Debit		Deposit		Balance	

Date Range ______________________ Balance Brought Forward $

Debit/ Check Number	Date	Description of Transaction	√	Withdrawal Amount/ Debit		Deposit		Balance	

Date Range ______________				Balance Brought Forward				$	
Debit/ Check Number	Date	Description of Transaction	√	Withdrawal Amount/ Debit		Deposit		Balance	

Date Range ______________________				Balance Brought Forward				$	
Debit/ Check Number	Date	Description of Transaction	√	Withdrawal Amount/ Debit		Deposit		Balance	

Date Range ______________________			Balance Brought Forward			$
Debit/ Check Number	Date	Description of Transaction	√	Withdrawal Amount/ Debit	Deposit	Balance

Date Range ______________________ | Balance Brought Forward | $

Debit/ Check Number	Date	Description of Transaction	√	Withdrawal Amount/ Debit		Deposit		Balance	

Date Range ______________			Balance Brought Forward					$	
Debit/ Check Number	Date	Description of Transaction	√	Withdrawal Amount/ Debit		Deposit		Balance	

Date Range ______________________				Balance Brought Forward				$	
Debit/ Check Number	Date	Description of Transaction	√	Withdrawal Amount/ Debit		Deposit		Balance	

Date Range ______________________				Balance Brought Forward				$	
Debit/ Check Number	Date	Description of Transaction	√	Withdrawal Amount/ Debit		Deposit		Balance	

Date Range ______________			Balance Brought Forward					$	
Debit/ Check Number	Date	Description of Transaction	√	Withdrawal Amount/ Debit		Deposit		Balance	

Date Range ________________				Balance Brought Forward		$
Debit/ Check Number	Date	Description of Transaction	√	Withdrawal Amount/ Debit	Deposit	Balance

Date Range ______________________				Balance Brought Forward				$	
Debit/ Check Number	Date	Description of Transaction	√	Withdrawal Amount/ Debit		Deposit		Balance	

Date Range ______________				Balance Brought Forward				$	
Debit/ Check Number	Date	Description of Transaction	√	Withdrawal Amount/ Debit		Deposit		Balance	

Date Range ______________________				Balance Brought Forward				$	
Debit/ Check Number	Date	Description of Transaction	√	Withdrawal Amount/ Debit		Deposit		Balance	

Date Range ____________				Balance Brought Forward				$	
Debit/ Check Number	Date	Description of Transaction	√	Withdrawal Amount/ Debit		Deposit		Balance	

Date Range ______________________				Balance Brought Forward				$	
Debit/ Check Number	Date	Description of Transaction	√	Withdrawal Amount/ Debit		Deposit		Balance	

Date Range ______________________ Balance Brought Forward $

Debit/ Check Number	Date	Description of Transaction	√	Withdrawal Amount/ Debit		Deposit		Balance	

Date Range ______________________			Balance Brought Forward					$	
Debit/ Check Number	Date	Description of Transaction	√	Withdrawal Amount/ Debit		Deposit		Balance	

Date Range ______________________ Balance Brought Forward $

Debit/ Check Number	Date	Description of Transaction	√	Withdrawal Amount/ Debit		Deposit		Balance	

Date Range ______________________				Balance Brought Forward				$	
Debit/ Check Number	Date	Description of Transaction	√	Withdrawal Amount/ Debit		Deposit		Balance	

Date Range ____________________ Balance Brought Forward $

Debit/ Check Number	Date	Description of Transaction	√	Withdrawal Amount/ Debit		Deposit		Balance	

Date Range ______________________				Balance Brought Forward				$	
Debit/ Check Number	Date	Description of Transaction	√	Withdrawal Amount/ Debit		Deposit		Balance	

Date Range ____________________ Balance Brought Forward $

Debit/ Check Number	Date	Description of Transaction	√	Withdrawal Amount/ Debit		Deposit		Balance	

Date Range ____________________ | Balance Brought Forward | $

Debit/ Check Number	Date	Description of Transaction	√	Withdrawal Amount/ Debit		Deposit		Balance	

Date Range ______________________				Balance Brought Forward				$	
Debit/ Check Number	Date	Description of Transaction	√	Withdrawal Amount/ Debit		Deposit		Balance	

Date Range ________________			Balance Brought Forward				$		
Debit/ Check Number	Date	Description of Transaction	√	Withdrawal Amount/ Debit		Deposit		Balance	

Date Range ____________________			Balance Brought Forward					$	
Debit/ Check Number	Date	Description of Transaction	√	Withdrawal Amount/ Debit		Deposit		Balance	

Date Range ____________________				Balance Brought Forward				$	
Debit/ Check Number	Date	Description of Transaction	√	Withdrawal Amount/ Debit		Deposit		Balance	

Date Range ______________________			Balance Brought Forward					$	
Debit/ Check Number	Date	Description of Transaction	√	Withdrawal Amount/ Debit		Deposit		Balance	

Date Range ____________________ | Balance Brought Forward | $

Debit/ Check Number	Date	Description of Transaction	√	Withdrawal Amount/ Debit		Deposit		Balance	

Date Range ______________________				Balance Brought Forward				$	
Debit/ Check Number	Date	Description of Transaction	√	Withdrawal Amount/ Debit		Deposit		Balance	

Date Range ____________________				Balance Brought Forward				$	
Debit/ Check Number	Date	Description of Transaction	√	Withdrawal Amount/ Debit		Deposit		Balance	

Date Range ____________________ | Balance Brought Forward $

Debit/ Check Number	Date	Description of Transaction	√	Withdrawal Amount/ Debit		Deposit		Balance	

Date Range ______________________				Balance Brought Forward			$		
Debit/ Check Number	Date	Description of Transaction	√	Withdrawal Amount/ Debit		Deposit		Balance	

Date Range ____________________				Balance Brought Forward				$	
Debit/ Check Number	Date	Description of Transaction	√	Withdrawal Amount/ Debit		Deposit		Balance	

Date Range ______________________			Balance Brought Forward					$	
Debit/ Check Number	Date	Description of Transaction	√	Withdrawal Amount/ Debit		Deposit		Balance	

Date Range ______________________ | Balance Brought Forward | $

Debit/ Check Number	Date	Description of Transaction	√	Withdrawal Amount/ Debit		Deposit		Balance	

Date Range ______________________				Balance Brought Forward				$	
Debit/ Check Number	Date	Description of Transaction	√	Withdrawal Amount/ Debit		Deposit		Balance	

Date Range ____________________				Balance Brought Forward				$	
Debit/ Check Number	Date	Description of Transaction	√	Withdrawal Amount/ Debit		Deposit		Balance	

Date Range ____________________			Balance Brought Forward				$		
Debit/ Check Number	Date	Description of Transaction	√	Withdrawal Amount/ Debit		Deposit		Balance	

Date Range ______________________ Balance Brought Forward $

Debit/ Check Number	Date	Description of Transaction	√	Withdrawal Amount/ Debit		Deposit		Balance	

Date Range ____________________				Balance Brought Forward				$	
Debit/ Check Number	Date	Description of Transaction	√	Withdrawal Amount/ Debit		Deposit		Balance	

Date Range ______________________			Balance Brought Forward					$	
Debit/ Check Number	Date	Description of Transaction	√	Withdrawal Amount/ Debit		Deposit		Balance	

Date Range ______________________ Balance Brought Forward $

Debit/ Check Number	Date	Description of Transaction	√	Withdrawal Amount/ Debit		Deposit		Balance	

Date Range ______________________ Balance Brought Forward $

Debit/ Check Number	Date	Description of Transaction	√	Withdrawal Amount/ Debit		Deposit		Balance	

Date Range ____________________			Balance Brought Forward				$		
Debit/ Check Number	Date	Description of Transaction	√	Withdrawal Amount/ Debit		Deposit		Balance	

Date Range ______________________ Balance Brought Forward $

Debit/ Check Number	Date	Description of Transaction	√	Withdrawal Amount/ Debit		Deposit		Balance	

Date Range ______________________			Balance Brought Forward				$		
Debit/ Check Number	Date	Description of Transaction	√	Withdrawal Amount/ Debit		Deposit		Balance	

Date Range ____________________ Balance Brought Forward $

Debit/ Check Number	Date	Description of Transaction	√	Withdrawal Amount/ Debit		Deposit		Balance	

Date Range ______________________							Balance Brought Forward	$	
Debit/ Check Number	Date	Description of Transaction	√	Withdrawal Amount/ Debit		Deposit		Balance	

Date Range ______________________ | Balance Brought Forward | $

Debit/ Check Number	Date	Description of Transaction	√	Withdrawal Amount/ Debit		Deposit		Balance	

Date Range ______________________			Balance Brought Forward				$		
Debit/ Check Number	Date	Description of Transaction	√	Withdrawal Amount/ Debit		Deposit		Balance	

Date Range ____________				Balance Brought Forward				$	
Debit/ Check Number	Date	Description of Transaction	√	Withdrawal Amount/ Debit		Deposit		Balance	

Date Range ______________________				Balance Brought Forward				$		
Debit/ Check Number	Date	Description of Transaction	√	Withdrawal Amount/ Debit		Deposit		Balance		

Date Range ______________________			Balance Brought Forward					$	
Debit/ Check Number	Date	Description of Transaction	√	Withdrawal Amount/ Debit		Deposit		Balance	

Date Range ____________________			Balance Brought Forward					$	
Debit/ Check Number	Date	Description of Transaction	√	Withdrawal Amount/ Debit		Deposit		Balance	

Date Range ____________________ Balance Brought Forward $

Debit/ Check Number	Date	Description of Transaction	√	Withdrawal Amount/ Debit		Deposit		Balance	

Date Range ______________________			Balance Brought Forward					$	
Debit/ Check Number	Date	Description of Transaction	√	Withdrawal Amount/ Debit		Deposit		Balance	

Date Range ________________			Balance Brought Forward					$	
Debit/ Check Number	Date	Description of Transaction	√	Withdrawal Amount/ Debit		Deposit		Balance	

Date Range ______________________ | Balance Brought Forward | $

Debit/ Check Number	Date	Description of Transaction	√	Withdrawal Amount/ Debit		Deposit		Balance	

Date Range ______________________				Balance Brought Forward				$	
Debit/ Check Number	Date	Description of Transaction	√	Withdrawal Amount/ Debit		Deposit		Balance	

Date Range ______________________				Balance Brought Forward				$	
Debit/ Check Number	Date	Description of Transaction	√	Withdrawal Amount/ Debit		Deposit		Balance	

Date Range ______________________				Balance Brought Forward		$
Debit/ Check Number	Date	Description of Transaction	√	Withdrawal Amount/ Debit	Deposit	Balance

Date Range ____________________			Balance Brought Forward					$	
Debit/ Check Number	Date	Description of Transaction	√	Withdrawal Amount/ Debit		Deposit		Balance	

Date Range ______________________ Balance Brought Forward $

Debit/ Check Number	Date	Description of Transaction	√	Withdrawal Amount/ Debit		Deposit		Balance	

Date Range ____________________ Balance Brought Forward $

Debit/ Check Number	Date	Description of Transaction	√	Withdrawal Amount/ Debit		Deposit		Balance	

Date Range ______________				Balance Brought Forward				$	
Debit/ Check Number	Date	Description of Transaction	√	Withdrawal Amount/ Debit		Deposit		Balance	

www.ingramcontent.com/pod-product-compliance
Lightning Source LLC
Chambersburg PA
CBHW081006170526
45158CB00010B/2926
9781081908331